PROPHETIC PATRIOTISM

A New Call to Action

Pastor Dominic Francese

PROPHETIC PATRIOTISM
A New Call to Action

ISBN: 978-1-949106-96-1

Published by Word and Spirit Publishing
P.O. Box 701403
Tulsa, Oklahoma 74170
wordandspiritpublishing.com

Dedication

To my wonderful wife, Kim. As was said to me by a co-worker in 1986 on the day of our wedding, "God didn't just give you a wife. He gave you a life." God's best life for me.

Contents

Introduction

What Do I Mean by "Prophetic Patriotism"?

Whose side are you on?

This seems to be the question that best defines the times in which we live. But I believe I have a different take on how American Christians should approach the issue.

The Bible, and the creeds of historical Christianity, tell us that Jesus promised to return to earth to rule and reign as its King. This is confirmed by passages like Matthew 24 and Acts 1, and by a reciting of the well-known Apostles' Creed ("He will come again in glory to judge the living and the dead, and His kingdom will have no end."). With this in mind, I will begin by sharing a metaphor.

Picture ten bowling pins, standing upright at the end of a bowling lane, waiting for a champion bowler to send down his ball for the game-winning strike. What is it that set those pins in place for this game-ending frame? The pinsetter, the mechanical device known to every bowler. It comes down from "above," sets all the pins in their proper configuration, and then disappears, up and out of sight.

The days described in the Bible as those immediately preceding the return of Jesus Christ are commonly referred to as the last days or the end times. Even though the United States of America is not specifically named among the biblical end times players and events predicted to "take the stage" before this Second Coming of Christ, the United States is nevertheless very much like the pinsetter that configures the pins in a bowling alley. In my analogy, the champion bowler represents God the Father, who is getting ready to send down His Son, Jesus Christ, for His promised return to rule and reign. Thanks to the Father's pinsetter, the United States, it will be a perfect strike. I have singled out ten biblically predicted end times "eye-openers" as being especially important. They are the "ten pins." Their placement on the world stage today has undeniably been brought about primarily by the United States of America.

This truth is so profound that I believe it compels us toward the following conclusion: God's hand was involved in the founding of America, to eventually bring about its end times prophetic role. What is America's ultimate purpose? It is now, to usher in the Second Coming of our Lord Jesus Christ.

If I am right, then right-of-center Christians should resist viewing American history only through the lens of a heroic narrative. Neither should left-of-center Christians think of American history as being blame-worthy. Instead, our history should be understood as being driven by a *prophetic* purpose, namely, that of being God's pinsetter. "Salvation is of the Jews" (John 4:22 KJV). But, setting the stage for the end times is the work of the United States.

Prophetic patriotism comes from the eye-opening realization that the time has come to stand up for a truly constitutional America, so that our last days assignment from God will not be lost. It is patriotism motivated by a passionate desire to see America fulfill its prophetic purpose!

Whose side are you on?

It is my hope that, after reading this book, you will agree that it is best to be on the side of biblical prophecy—God's side.

1

Defender of the Jews

Pin #1: Israel

If we want to understand America's role as God's pinsetter, the best place to begin is in the Gospel of Luke. So, let's go there first.

When Jesus approached Jerusalem, He saw the city and wept over it. Then, with a tear in His eye, He said the following:

> *"If you had known on this day, even you, the conditions for peace! But now they have been hidden*

> *from your eyes. For the days will come upon you when your enemies will put up a barricade against you, and surround you and hem you in on every side, and they will level you to the ground, and throw down your children within you, and they will not leave in you one stone upon another, because you did not recognize the time of your visitation."*
>
> —LUKE 19:42–44

Jesus continued, speaking of the land of Israel and the Jewish people:

> *"For there will be great distress upon the land, and wrath to this people; and they will fall by the edge of the sword, and will be led captive into all the nations; and Jerusalem will be trampled under-foot by the Gentiles until the times of the Gentiles are fulfilled."*
>
> —LUKE 21:23B–24

Jesus' words literally came true. After the fall of Jerusalem at the hands of the Romans in 70 A.D., the "times of the Gentiles" stretched from the beginning of the dispersion of the Jewish people, referred to as the

Diaspora, until the retaking of the Temple Mount by the Israeli army during the 1967 Six-Day War.

But what is it that precipitated the Jews' return to their land, after almost two thousand years of being scattered among the nations? To answer this question, consider the words of Jesus. In Luke 24:44, Jesus states that all must be fulfilled that was written about Him in the Old Testament. In addition, historical Christianity strongly asserts that the predictions of the Old Testament prophets were given by the Spirit of God and will come to pass sooner or later. (The Apostle's Creed clearly states that the Holy Spirit spoke through the prophets.) With this in mind, the Bible says that God gave the prophet Ezekiel a picture over five hundred years before Christ that tells us what would precipitate the Jews' return to their land in modern times. It is known as the "Valley of Dry Bones." Let's read some of it, understanding that in the Old Testament, to be "cut off" meant to be "killed":

Then He said to me, "Son of man, these bones are the entire house of Israel; behold, they say, 'Our

> *bones are dried up and our hope has perished. We are completely cut off.'"*
>
> —EZEKIEL 37:11

Can we know what is being symbolically predicted by the glimpse into the future that we just read? Let's answer that question by asking another: When in modern history did the hope of the Jewish nation seem to perish, and when were they "completely cut off"? These events occurred during the Nazi Holocaust. By the Nazi Holocaust, I mean the unspeakable, horrific attempt by Hitler and his henchmen to exterminate the Jewish people during World War II. Through Ezekiel, I believe God was saying that this event, the Holocaust, would finally precipitate the return of the Jews to their land. We see this in what God said next to Ezekiel, as the prophet is told to speak to the dry bones:

> *Therefore, prophesy and say to them, 'This is what the Lord God says: "Behold, I am going to open your graves and cause you to come up out of your graves, my people; and I will bring you into the land of Israel."*
>
> —EZEKIEL 37:12

And so, it came to pass. The reestablishment of the State of Israel took place in 1948, shortly after World War II.

However, "the Valley of Dry Bones" representing the Holocaust, is not to say persecution of the Jews at that time was something new. The Jewish people had experienced persecution for almost two thousand years! But one nation was the exception, the place where the Jews were safe. Which nation was this?

Let's recall the analogy with the pinsetter and the first bowling pin: Before the Second Coming, there needed to be a safe haven for the first pin which is Israel. That safe haven has been the pinsetter, not named in Scripture, but present nevertheless: the United States of America.

George Washington himself firmly established that America would be a "friend to the Jew" with a specific letter he sent to a Jewish congregation in Rhode Island in response to the petition they sent him. They explained they had been persecuted by other nations, and now they had come to America hoping for a safe home. They questioned whether this country was going to be any different. George Washington's letter has been a national treasure to the American Jewish community for over two hundred years. Here's a portion of what he said, referring to the U.S. Constitution as the government of the United States:

> *The government of the United States...gives to bigotry no sanction, and to persecution no assistance.... May the children of the stock of Abraham who dwell in this land continue to merit and enjoy the good will of [its] other inhabitants, while every one [of you] shall sit in safety under his vine and under his fig tree, and there shall be no one to make him afraid.*
>
> —Letter to the Jews of Newport from George Washington

America has been a safe haven for the Jewish people. But God's defender nation would not only have to be willing to protect the Jews during the Diaspora, but also be willing to defend a newly established State of Israel. That new Jewish nation would rise again, like Ezekiel's dry bones, from horrific persecution, to new life as a God-ordained nation. God's defender nation would have to be strong enough to protect them during the process of their rebirth, when no other nation would do so.

Even though the reestablishment of the State of Israel in 1948 was met with worldwide anger, the United States stood strong for the Jews. And the support of the United States was invaluable in this reestablishment. By 1948, the United States had established itself as a world superpower with its victory in World War II, and it could use its influence to guide world events to assist in Israel's rebirth. The timing of the U.S. ascendency was not an accident!

But that was then. This is now. Is America still willing to be God's defender of the Jewish nation? If the answer is no, will Israel still be protected? The Old Testament book of Esther provides an answer.

The events of the book of Esther happened over four hundred years before Christ. The Jews had been exiled by the Babylonian Empire, but the subsequent Medo-Persian Empire had allowed them to return to their land. Although some had done so, many other Jews remained scattered throughout the provinces of the new empire. God sovereignly elevated one of them, Esther, to be queen of that empire. But the king had a high official named Haman, who hated Esther's uncle, Mordecai, who worked in the palace alongside Haman. Because of his hatred for Mordecai, Haman arranged to have all of the Jews killed, throughout the empire, on a certain future date. He did this, not knowing that the queen was Jewish, or that Mordecai was Esther's uncle.

As recorded in the Old Testament, after Haman's plot was set in motion, Mordecai appealed to Esther to go to the king and plead for the lives of her people before it was too late.

> *Then Mordecai told them to reply to Esther, "Do not imagine that you in the king's palace can escape any more than all the other Jews. For if you keep silent at this time, liberation and rescue will arise for the Jews from another place, and you and your father's house will perish. And who knows whether you have not attained royalty for such a time as this?"*
>
> —ESTHER 4:13–14

I believe this admonition can be applied to our nation today. Just take out "Esther" and put "America" in her place. God will protect Israel. If America's heavenly mandate is to defend Israel in our time, and we don't do what God raised us up to do, we risk the destruction of the United States. The Bible says that Esther found her courage and defended the Jewish people. It is my hope and prayer that we as a nation will keep our courage and continue to do the same.

Applying Mordecai's admonition on an individual level, this also means that if there's anything you personally might say or do that prevents the United States from supporting Israel, please think twice about it. God has a plan. Following His plan is always the wisest course of action! It doesn't turn out well for those who resist His plan.

As an example of this personal application, consider that God "cut a covenant" with Abraham, the founder of the Jewish nation, as recorded in the book of Genesis.

> *But he said, "LORD GOD, how may I know that I will possess it?" So He said to him, "Bring Me a three-year-old heifer, a three-year-old female*

goat, a three-year-old ram, a turtledove, and a young pigeon." Then he brought all these to Him and cut them in two, and laid each half opposite the other; but he did not cut the birds. And birds of prey came down upon the carcasses, and Abram drove them away.

Now when the sun was going down, a deep sleep fell upon Abram; and behold, terror and great darkness fell upon him. Then God said to Abram, "Know for certain that your descendants will be strangers in a land that is not theirs, where they will be enslaved and oppressed for four hundred years. But I will also judge the nation whom they will serve, and afterward they will come out with many possessions. As for you, you shall go to your fathers in peace; you will be buried at a good old age. Then in the fourth generation they will return here, for the wrongdoing of the Amorite is not yet complete."

Now it came about, when the sun had set, that it was very dark, and behold, a smoking oven and a flaming torch appeared which passed between these pieces. On that day the L*ORD* *made a covenant with Abram, saying,*

"To your descendants I have given this land,
From the river of Egypt as far as the great river,
the river Euphrates."

—GENESIS 15:8–18

In this passage, a ritual is described which required that animals be split in two with both halves laid opposite from one another. The two people agreeing to the covenant were required to walk between the two halves. This was an ancient way of saying, "May the fate of that animal come upon me if I fail to keep the promise of this agreement." Author Hal Lindsey gives a good explanation of this in his book, *The Everlasting Hatred*. In the Genesis 15 narrative, God Himself came down in front of Abraham, in the form of fire, and "passed between the pieces." But Abraham did not do likewise. God never asked Abraham to do the same. In this way, the agreement was unconditional. The promise that God made was to give the land of Israel to Abraham's descendants, the Jewish people. This act was also a confirmation that God would indeed "bless those who bless Abraham's descendants, and curse those who curse them":

> *Now the LORD said to Abram,*
>
> *"Go from your country,*
> *And from your relatives*
> *And from your father's house,*
> *To the land which I will show you;*
> *And I will make you into a great nation,*
> *And I will bless you,*
> *And make your name great;*
> *And you shall be a blessing;*
> *And I will bless those who bless you,*
> *And the one who curses you I will curse.*
> *And in you all the families of the earth will be blessed."*
>
> —GENESIS 12:1–3

In keeping with this Abrahamic covenant, it could be that President Trump failed to return to the White House in 2020 because of his "Deal of the Century," proposed in January of that same year. The deal was Trump's diplomatic initiative to establish peace in the Middle East. The proposal stated that some of

Abraham's land should be given to the Palestinians. President Trump had been a great friend to Israel up to that point, and this brought about a blessing upon his presidency and prosperity for the country despite great opposition. However, his Deal of the Century inadvertently set him at cross-purposes with God. It could be that the above-mentioned "curse" took effect, and election irregularities that could have been stopped by the hand of God were not.

I do understand that God can cause what happened in 2020 to "work together for good" as stated in Romans 8:28, especially regarding the uncovering of corruption and the galvanizing of the righteous. But if President Trump was ever to return to the White House, and if I was ever given an open door to talk to him about this, I would respectfully ask him to please never again affirm anyone else's right to Abraham's land. In God's eyes, it is the land of the Jewish people, and keeping it that way is a big part of America's prophetic purpose.

2

Reunited in Democracy

Pin #2: Roman Empire 2.0

After World War II, Europe desperately needed help. The war had devastated the entire continent. And the program the United States implemented at that time, whereby a treasure trove of American dollars was voluntarily spent to help Europe rebuild, was called the Marshall Plan.

What were the aftereffects of the Marshall Plan? For one thing, after hundreds of years, all of Europe was finally pressured into committing to democratic forms of government rather than instituting kings or embracing fascism. In addition, the tracks were laid for Pan-European multinational structures, including NATO and the European Union. For the first time since the time of the Caesars, the territory of the old Roman Empire was again beginning to function as one entity, albeit through partially strong and partially weak governments.

Biblical prophecy speaks about a "Roman Empire 2.0" emerging just before Christ's return. In keeping with this, after World War II, Europe needed an influence strong enough to help its partially weak and partially strong multiple governments democratize and function together. That strong influence has turned out to be the United States.

To understand this Roman Empire 2.0 prediction in the Bible, we must turn back the clock to a time more than five hundred years before Christ. This was the time of another empire called the Babylonian Empire. Its first king was a man named Nebuchadnezzar. As we join his story, he is having a very disturbing dream. Let's pick up the narrative in Daniel, chapter 2, verse 25. I included the headings of the New American Standard Bible, which represent commonly held beliefs surrounding the meaning of the symbols in this dream.

> *Then Arioch hurriedly brought Daniel into the king's presence and spoke to him as follows: "I have found a man among the exiles from Judah who can make the interpretation known to the king!" The king said to Daniel, whose name was Belteshazzar, "Are you able to make known to me the dream which I have seen and its interpretation?" Daniel answered before the king and said, "As for the secret about which the king has inquired, neither wise men, sorcerers, soothsayer priests, nor diviners are able to declare it to the king. However, there is a God in heaven who reveals secrets, and He has made known to King Nebuchadnezzar what will take place in the latter days. This was your dream and the visions in your mind while on your bed. As for you, O king, while on your bed your thoughts turned to what would take place in the future; and He who reveals secrets has made known to you what will take place. But as for me, this secret has not been revealed to me for any wisdom residing in me more than in any other living person, but for the*

purpose of making the interpretation known to the king, and that you may understand the thoughts of your mind.

The King's Dream

"You, O king, were watching and behold, there was a single great statue; that statue, which was large and of extraordinary radiance, was standing in front of you, and its appearance was awesome. The head of that statue was made of fine gold, its chest and its arms of silver, its belly and its thighs of bronze, its legs of iron, and its feet partly of iron and partly of clay. You continued watching until a stone was broken off without hands, and it struck the statue on its feet of iron and clay, and crushed them. Then the iron, the clay, the bronze, the silver, and the gold were crushed to pieces all at the same time, and they were like chaff from the summer threshing floors; and the wind carried them away so that not a trace of them was found. But the stone that struck the statue became a great mountain and filled the entire earth."

The Interpretation—Babylon the First Kingdom

"This was the dream; and now we will tell its interpretation before the king. You, O king, are the king of kings, to whom the God of heaven has given the kingdom, the power, the strength, and the honor; and wherever the sons of mankind live, or the animals of the field, or the birds of the sky, He has handed them over to you and has made you ruler over them all. You are the head of gold."

Medo-Persia and Greece

"And after you another kingdom will arise inferior to you, then another third kingdom of bronze, which will rule over all the earth."

Rome

"Then there will be a fourth kingdom as strong as iron; just as iron smashes and crushes everything, so, like iron that crushes, it will smash and crush all these things. And in that you saw the feet and toes, partly of potter's clay and partly of iron, it will be a divided kingdom; but it will have within

it some of the toughness of iron, since you saw the iron mixed with common clay. And just as the toes of the feet were partly of iron and partly of pottery, so some of the kingdom will be strong, and part of it will be fragile. In that you saw the iron mixed with common clay, they will combine with one another in their descendants; but they will not adhere to one another, just as iron does not combine with pottery."

The Divine Kingdom

"And in the days of those kings the God of heaven will set up a kingdom which will never be destroyed, and that kingdom will not be left for another people; it will crush and put an end to all these kingdoms, but it will itself endure forever. Just as you saw that a stone was broken off from the mountain without hands, and that it crushed the iron, the bronze, the clay, the silver, and the gold, the great God has made known to the king what will take place in the future; so the dream is certain and its interpretation is trustworthy."

—DANIEL 2:25–45

The strong and united legs in Daniel's prophecy, which indicate the old Roman Empire, are history. But the divided and weaker version of that empire, with iron and clay feet, is a future state or empire. It is the Roman Empire 2.0. It was the Marshall Plan and its aftermath that finally revealed the role the United States was meant to play in bringing about the "feet portion" of Daniel's prophecy.

But why would the Roman Empire, in particular, have to be reborn before the Second Coming of Christ? I believe this will happen for the purpose of biblical reciprocity.

When I say "biblical reciprocity," I'm referring to a principle actually found throughout Scripture. For example, consider these instructions: "An eye for an eye, a tooth for a tooth" from Exodus 21:24; "Give, and it shall be given unto you" from Luke 6:38; "With the measure that you mete, it shall be measured back to you again" from Mark 4:24. These verses indicate the principle of reciprocity. In the case of the Roman Empire, Christ died at the hands of Rome. And now, at His Second Coming, which is understood by biblical scholars to be the stone in Daniel's prophecy, Rome will die at the hands of Christ.

And why was the United States also destined to be the democratizer, or the enabler, of a "common clay" version of Rome? To start, in my opinion, clay represents the votes of common people. America would be the democratizer of Rome 2.0 so that a bureaucratic template could be created for a future *world government*. In other words, I believe this partly weak and partly strong Roman Empire, made up of different countries, will be the model that will ultimately help all nations to function as one global entity. We will return to this idea later.

3

Enmity Yet to Come

Pin #3: The Future Antichrist

Pin #4: A "Future Eve"

We've been seeing things take place in our lifetimes that no one who lived before us could have ever imagined: satellites, cell phones, laptops, emails, texts, and social media. And who gave the world this "Digital Age"? The United States.

Here are two more pins in the bowling pin analogy. In addition to what we've already seen, I believe America is destined to be the catalyst for both the future Antichrist, and a "Future Eve." You've probably heard about the coming Antichrist, but what do I mean by a "Future Eve"?

God created the first human beings in the Garden of Eden. It was there that Eve, along with her husband, Adam, disobeyed God at the urging of Satan. Immediately afterward, God spoke directly to both Satan and Eve. Let's see what He said:

> *"I [God] will put enmity between thee and the woman, and between thy seed and her seed; it shall bruise thy head, and thou shalt bruise his heel."*
>
> —GENESIS 3:15 (KJV)

Obviously, the "thee" here is referring to Satan, and "the woman" is referring to Eve. The woman's "seed," eventually coming through the Virgin Mary, is prophetically speaking of Jesus Christ. But who is the "seed" of the serpent, Satan?

Consider the temptation of Adam and Eve in Genesis 3.

> *The serpent said to the woman, "You certainly will not die! For God knows that on the day you eat from it your eyes will be opened, and you will become like God, knowing good and evil."*
>
> —GENESIS 3:4–5

Satan said: If you disobey God, then you will be like God. In other words, Satan claimed that Adam and Eve would essentially *be* God on the earth, if they simply *disobeyed* God.

And so they did.

Since that time, people have responded to Satan by saying, "Yes, we agree with you." The result has been that all people who came after Adam and Eve have been born with a natural selfishness called sin. 1 Corinthians highlights the fact that we all die spiritually because of that first sin.

> *For as in Adam all die, so also in Christ all will be made alive.*
>
> —1 Corinthians 15:22

One byproduct of this fallen, sinful nature is that people collectively became pawns in Satan's scheme to dominate the world. After all, God gave people rulership over the whole earth as explained earlier in Genesis:

> *God blessed them; and God said to them, "Be fruitful and multiply, and fill the earth, and subdue it; and rule over the fish of the sea and over the birds of the sky and over every living thing that moves on the earth."*
>
> —Genesis 1:28

By obeying Satan, they submitted to his authority and turned away from God's authority. It was the beginning of the great tug-of-war that now operates in the heart of all people as they experience the desire to fulfill the eternal purpose placed within them by God but succumb to the lie that is held before them, believing they must preserve themselves. Adam and Eve relinquished their rulership to Satan when they submitted to him and agreed to his plan. They gave up their authority over the earth, and Satan took it. His intent is one-world domination, through people who are still willing to go along with his plan and call themselves "god" of their own destiny. That's why the Bible predicts that a one-world government is coming, under the dictatorship of a so-called Antichrist who will claim to be God.

Here's how the apostle Paul described the coming Antichrist:

> *No one is to deceive you in any way! For it [the Second Coming of Christ] will not come unless the apostasy comes first, and the man of lawlessness is revealed, the son of destruction, who opposes and exalts himself above every so-called god or object of worship, so that he takes his seat in the temple of God, displaying himself as being God.*
>
> —2 THESSALONIANS 2:3–4

This is how the apostle John described the future reign of this person, here called the "beast," in the book of Revelation:

> *And he causes all, the small and the great, the rich and the poor, and the free and the slaves, to be given a mark on their right hands or on their foreheads, and he decrees that no one will be able to buy or to sell, except the one who has the mark, either the name of the beast or the number of his name.*
>
> —Revelation 13:16–17

The future buy-and-sell scenario John described was impossible until the Digital Age. Today, it's not only possible—it's "here." The banking systems of the entire world are joined together by satellites orbiting the earth. They are digitally connected. When thinking about economic controls placed on people, consider the Covid-19 pandemic and the protest displayed in Canada by a convoy of truck drivers. Their bank accounts were frozen by the government. The technology-enabled controls that were put in place during the pandemic have prepared the way for a future banking system that can control economic freedom for select groups of people. In the same way, the dictator called the Antichrist will be ready to freeze the accounts of any who disagree with him.

So, what else do we know about this future dictator "beast"? Let's read further:

> *"Then the king will do as he pleases, and he will exalt himself and boast against every god and will speak dreadful things against the God of gods; and he will be successful until the indignation is finished, because that which is determined will be done. And he will show no regard for the gods of his fathers or for the desire of women, nor will he show regard for any other god; for he will boast against them all."*
>
> —DANIEL 11:35–37

Did you catch that? "No regard for the desire of women." I believe this means that he will not think of them as precious, and he will disregard what they desire. I don't believe this is saying he won't be heterosexual, since that would offend many religious people across the world that Scripture says will one day follow the Antichrist. But, why would this "beast" hate women?

To answer that question, let's look at something else that God showed John in the book of Revelation.

> *And I saw another angel flying in midheaven with an eternal gospel to preach to those who live on the earth, and to every nation, tribe, language, and people; and he said with a loud voice, "Fear God and give Him glory, because the hour of His judgment has come; worship Him who made the heaven and the earth, and sea and springs of waters." And another angel, a second one, followed, saying, "Fallen, fallen is Babylon the great, she who has made all the nations drink of the wine of the passion of her sexual immorality." Then another angel, a third one, followed them, saying with a loud voice, "If anyone worships the beast and his image, and receives a mark on his forehead or on his hand, he also will drink of the wine of the wrath of God, which is mixed in full strength in the cup of His anger; and he will be tormented with fire and brimstone in the presence of the holy angels and in the presence of the Lamb."*
>
> —REVELATION 14:6–10

But wait a minute. Look at the beginning of that passage of Scripture. Angelic beings aren't supposed to preach the Gospel. *Human beings* are the ones who received the Great Commission from Jesus. The Great Commission is the assignment to preach the Gospel, the Good News about Himself, to the whole world as shown in the book of Matthew.

> *And Jesus came up and spoke to them, saying, "All authority in heaven and on earth has been given to Me. Go, therefore, and make disciples of all the nations, baptizing them in the name of the Father and the Son and the Holy Spirit, teaching them to follow all that I commanded you; and behold, I am with you always, to the end of the age."*
>
> —MATTHEW 28:18–20

Notice that Jesus took back the authority that was given to Satan. Those who follow Jesus are no longer operating under the sin nature passed down by Adam and Eve. They have been born again with a new spirit that is connected to the Holy Spirit of God. As they live through the spirit-to-Spirit connection, the tug-of-war of the heart is finished, and they are free to obey Jesus and make disciples, baptize them, and teach them. But, is John saying that, in the future, God will change His mind and suddenly tell an angel to carry out the Great

Commission? I don't think so. Along those lines, didn't we just read that *one* angel will supposedly speak *to every nation*? How can just one angel do that?

I don't believe the passage in Revelation was actually speaking of an angelic being "flying in midheaven." *Angelos*, the original Greek word used here, means not only "angel," but also "messenger." I believe God was actually showing John a "messenger" in the atmosphere. That messenger could be referring to a *communications satellite*, a "messenger" preaching the Gospel. A communications satellite would have been a messenger with which John was unfamiliar. And not only was it conveying the "eternal Gospel" to every nation, which one satellite can certainly do, but it was also a mechanism to warn people that the man demanding to be worshipped is the long-predicted Antichrist, so do not follow him!

Today, many would say Big Tech blocks any information the political ruling class directs them to block, including some online Christian content. But that is only causing alternative platforms to spring up. The new platforms will allow Christians to communicate through social media, and John's "messenger" is the means by which the social media communications will operate and the Gospel will be preached.

I believe Revelation 14 indicates that God will give wisdom to His people during the reign of the Antichrist, enabling them to get around any attempts to stop the digital spread of the Gospel. There won't be anything the "beast" will be able to do about it, unless he takes *all* the satellites out of the sky. But if he did that, he would be shutting down his own means of control, namely, the world's banking system. Again, it could be that Revelation 14 is predicting that there *will* continue to be "social media for Jesus" in the days of the Antichrist. And it will be a no-win situation for him.

What does the "messenger" satellite have to do with Eve and today's women?

The prediction in Genesis about Satan and the woman was pointing to the Virgin Mary and the birth of Jesus, but could it be that it was also pointing to *a* "Future Eve"? Is there a generation of women who will be a digital hindrance to the Antichrist? Currently, women use social media more than men. Could it be that the phrase from Genesis, "I [God] will put enmity [hatred] between you and the woman," was speaking prophetically about women using social media during the last days to hinder Satan? The "beast" is the predicted "seed of the serpent." He will hate women for hindering him. But the "Future Eve" will prevail. Why? Because again, biblical reciprocity demands it: Satan got the best of Eve in the Garden at the beginning. Eve will get the best of Satan in the end. I call it "Eve's revenge."

Women can be encouraged as they read the apostle John's letters to the Christians of his day. By extension, his words were written to us as well. Here's some of what he said:

> *Children, it is the last hour; and just as you heard that antichrist is coming, even now many antichrists have appeared; from this we know that it is the last hour. They went out from us, but they were not really of us; for if they had been of us, they would have remained with us; but they went out, so that it would be evident that they all are not of us. But you have an anointing from the Holy One, and you all know.*
>
> —1 JOHN 2:18–20

Women of God, you have an anointing from God which includes a prophecy, a promise made to you back in the Garden of Eden. The apostle John is saying you don't have to wait for the future—you can start now. You've already been empowered to take the authority God has prophetically given you. You've already been given the wisdom to effectively use the tools and platforms that He has placed at your disposal. The time is now!

4

The Power Vacuum

Pin #5: The Rapture's Aftermath

Pin #6: The Russian Invasion

The Bible teaches that the end of human history will be like "birth pangs," labor pains leading up to the "birth" of the Second Coming of Christ (Matthew 24:8). We can't know all the details, but we know this period will be a very difficult time, and at the conclusion of these days, Jesus will come again to rule the world in peace (Matthew 24:30; 25:34).

Even though the Scriptures often use symbolism to describe the final days, some descriptions are actually quite specific. For example, the Bible says there's a day coming, a day just like today, when the sun rises and the birds start singing, when Jesus will return for the purpose of receiving His church. I agree with those who say this event will happen in the sky as described in 1 Thessalonians.

> *Then we who are alive, who remain, will be caught up together with them in the clouds to meet the Lord in the air, and so we will always be with the Lord.*
>
> —1 THESSALONIANS 4:17

Scripture also tells us that Jesus will return to the earth itself, to the mountain outside Jerusalem where He left His disciples:

> *And as they were gazing intently into the sky while He was going, then behold, two men in white clothing stood beside them, and they said, "Men of Galilee, why do you stand looking into the sky? This Jesus, who has been taken up from you into*

heaven, will come in the same way as you have watched Him go into heaven." Then they returned to Jerusalem from the mountain called Olivet, which is near Jerusalem.

—ACTS 1:10–12

I agree with those who say the event of Jesus coming to receive His church in the sky will happen at least seven years before His return to that mountain, to reign on the earth.

Developing further this idea of two returns, Jesus said we cannot know the day or the hour of His coming (Matthew 24:36). But the book of Revelation, for example, says that the last half of the final seven years before His return will take place over a specific number of days.

And I will grant authority to my two witnesses, and they will prophesy for 1,260 days, clothed in sackcloth.

—REVELATION 11:3

Since a total number of days was just specifically stated, and yet Jesus said we cannot know the day or hour of His coming, it follows that there must be two separate events of Jesus returning.

When Jesus comes in the sky for His church, those of us who believe in Him will instantly be caught up with Him. More specifically, according to Scripture, we will receive our resurrection bodies and instantly go to heaven. Here's how the apostle Paul explained it in two of his letters to the early church:

> *Behold, I am telling you a mystery; we will not all sleep, but we will all be changed, in a moment, in the twinkling of an eye, at the last trumpet; for the trumpet will sound, and the dead will be raised imperishable, and we will be changed.*
>
> —1 CORINTHIANS 15:51–52

> *For we say this to you by the word of the Lord, that we who are alive and remain until the coming of the Lord will not precede those who have fallen asleep. For the Lord Himself will descend from heaven with a shout, with the voice of the archangel and with the trumpet of God, and the dead in Christ will rise first. Then we who are alive, who*

remain, will be caught up together with them in the clouds to meet the Lord in the air, and so we will always be with the Lord. Therefore, comfort one another with these words.

—1 THESSALONIANS 4:15–18

This event has become known as "the rapture." When that day comes, everyone left behind on earth will know it, and they will turn in bewilderment to God. That's why the enemy of our souls, Satan, is working overtime in the spiritual realm, trying to come up with a deception that will be big enough to explain-away the rapture. The enemy knows what's coming.

It has been widely publicized in recent years that 40 percent of American active-duty military personnel are evangelical Christians. Evangelical Christians typically look for opportunities to share Christ with others. While some might correct me by saying that military leaders with an anti-God agenda have used vaccine requirements as a way to weed out the sincerely religious, there is still a significant percentage of the military who can be identified as Christian. In fact, assuming all of the military's Spirit-filled believers would be raptured, it is still my guess that nearly 40 percent of our U.S. military would be taken into heaven if that day were to happen any time soon. The result would be a gutting of the U.S. military.

But there's another crucial sector of America's infrastructure widely known to be filled with faithful churchgoers—namely, farmers. They feed the United States citizens as well as a sizable percentage of the world's population. So, besides the military, if American farmers were to suddenly be taken away, global financial markets would panic. After all, the world's developing nations would immediately be on the brink of chaos because of massive food shortages. Just look at what the prospect of current food shortages is causing in the way of panic today.

But what about Spirit-filled Christians outside of America? According to Operation Mobilization, there are around one hundred million Christians in China today. But are they in places of power? Are they allowed to have places of importance in that nation's ability to function? No. If China's Christians were to be suddenly raptured from out of a population of over a billion, China would still be very powerful on the world stage.

By contrast, the gutting of America's military and the loss of our food supply would leave the United States crippled as a world power.

Looking at another example, a large number of Christian revival gatherings are going on in developing, non-industrialized countries right now. But similar to what is happening in China, the ones participating and coming to Christ are not the established or the well-to-do. They are often the poorest of the poor. Only in America would an infrastructure-crippling power vacuum take place if that day were to come today.

Two more pins: I believe the United States was destined by God to set up the rapture's global impact, and by extension, to set up the Russian move against the Antichrist predicted in Scripture.

Thinking logically, if the United States were to be eliminated as a superpower, which other nations would probably try to step in and fill that vacuum on the world stage? Russia and China.

In recent years, Vladimir Putin, the leader of Russia at the time of this writing, has publicly stated that his ultimate goal has been to reinstate "Great Russia."

He even called the breakup of the U.S.S.R., the Soviet Russian Empire, "the greatest geopolitical catastrophe of the twentieth century." His words, as further evidenced by the Ukrainian conflict he instigated, prove that the Soviet-era dream of Russian world domination never went away. If the rapture happens any time soon, Putin, or whoever is leading Russia at the time, might be relieved that America's power is gone, but still consider the Antichrist's power to be a challenge. As that Russian leader considers indirect ways to snatch world control away from him, I believe a light bulb will go on in that Russian chess-player's mind. Yes, there *is* a way. And that "way" has to do with the lifeblood of every industrialized nation's economy—energy.

Green energy initiatives do not change the fact that a complete removal of oil can collapse *any* industrialized nation's economy. That's why Russia is one day going to invade Israel, and then the entire Middle East, to get control of the vast reserves of oil in that region.

What follows is the way Ezekiel describes this invasion. I believe God spoke through Ezekiel in terms of horses, shields, and swords because the people of Ezekiel's day would not have understood mechanized warfare. But since this event has not yet come to pass, I do believe it is describing a last days battle.

> *Now the word of the LORD came to me, saying, "Son of man, set your face toward Gog of the land of Magog, the chief prince of Meshech and Tubal, and prophesy against him, and say, 'This is what the Lord GOD says: "Behold, I am against you, Gog, chief prince of Meshech and Tubal. So I will turn you around and put hooks into your jaws, and I will bring you out, and all your army, horses and horsemen, all of them magnificently dressed, a great contingent with shield and buckler, all of them wielding swords; Persia, Cush, and Put with them, all of them with buckler and helmet; Gomer with all its troops; Beth-togarmah from the remote parts of the north with all its troops; many peoples with you.*
>
> *"Be ready, and be prepared, you and all your contingents that are assembled around you, and be a guard for them. After many days you will be summoned; in the latter years you will come into the land that is restored from the sword, whose inhabitants have been gathered from many*

> *nations to the mountains of Israel which had been a continual place of ruins; but its people were brought out from the nations, and they are living securely, all of them. And you will go up, you will come like a storm; you will be like a cloud covering the land, you and all your troops, and many peoples with you."*
>
> —EZEKIEL 38:1–9

Dr. Alfred Edersheim, in his landmark seven-volume work *Bible History: Old Testament*, identified "Magog" as the people called Scythians, who occupied what is today Southern Russia. "Magog" also speaks of the area of present-day Russia, according to the ancient Jewish historian Josephus. So, I do believe that "the land of Magog" in Ezekiel 38 is speaking of Russia.

But Ezekiel 38 tells us how that bold move will play out. This is God again speaking to Ezekiel:

> *"I will send fire upon Magog and those who inhabit the coastlands in safety; and they will know that I am the Lord."*
>
> —EZEKIEL 39:6

I believe this passage of Scripture indicates there will be an exchange of fire in the form of nuclear missiles between Russia and the United States with Magog represented as present-day Russia and the coastlands symbolizing the United States. Russia will suffer more, but the United States will also suffer. We cannot imagine the suffering on both sides, and so we should read this passage with a broken heart.

Remember that a bowling alley pinsetter sets pins in place and then disappears. In this case, the pinsetter, or the United States as the pinsetter, is going to literally disappear in large measure, and the subsequent impact will act as a catalyst for what follows. In other words, Christian America's disappearance will speed up the events, bringing current events to an end.

We are living in extremely consequential times, which have been foreordained by the wisdom of God to serve as proof to an unbelieving world that the Bible is true, and that mankind has not been left to his own devices. According to Jesus, the rapture could take place any day. Are you ready?

5

Kings from the East

Pin #7: The Rise of China

China is very much in the news today. But the roots of its news-making culture and mindset go back to the days of Genghis Kahn. In Jack Weatherford's book, *Genghis Kahn and the Making of the Modern World*, the author points out that Genghis Kahn believed that he was destined to rule the world. In my opinion, the current rulers in China believe the same. Let's look at the connection between Genghis Kahn and today's China.

Genghis Kahn was from Mongolia in Central Asia, situated between China and Russia. During his rulership, in the early 1200s, the widest extent of his empire stretched from Eastern Europe to the Pacific Coast of Northern China.

But Genghis Kahn did not conquer the lower half of China. It was his grandson Kublai Kahn who did so. It was he who moved the capital of that Mongolian empire to Beijing. And it was he who unified China into one nation within his empire, as opposed to a collection of various clans. Kublai Kahn called this land and its people, now hosting his capital city, the Yuan dynasty.

Today, China's capital is still Beijing. Its unit of currency is still called the Yuan. And the "belief" that it is China's destiny to one day rule the world still exists in China's national consciousness, along with the one-world vision of authoritarian communism.

In 1972, American President Richard Nixon shocked the world by visiting the closed, authoritarian People's Republic of China, allowing the free-market West to see images from inside that country for the first time since

World War II. This effectively brought China back into the post-World War II family of nations.

In 2001, the United States approved and paved the way for communist China to join the World Trade Organization, which up to that point had been led by capitalist America and the free-trade nations of Europe. What happened next was a transfer of wealth and technology into China such as had never been seen before. American multinational corporations soon became dependent on the cheap labor that China's one-billion-plus population provided. This dependency is still in place today, and to a much greater degree! That is why the China-spawned COVID-19 pandemic did not publicly place China at odds with the United States and Europe. China has become too powerful economically and technologically for that to have happened. China is now effectively the world's second greatest superpower, next to the United States. But China could not have achieved this status without the help of the United States of America.

According to the apostle John in the book of Revelation, just before the Second Coming of Christ, a very large army will march toward the Middle East. Here are two glimpses of this army from his words:

> *Then the sixth angel sounded, and I heard a voice from the four horns of the golden altar which is before God, saying to the sixth angel who had the trumpet, "Release the four angels who are bound at the great river Euphrates." And the four angels, who had been prepared for the hour and day and month and year, were released, so that they would kill a third of mankind. The number of the armies of the horsemen was two hundred million; I heard the number of them.*
>
> —Revelation 9:13–16

The book of Revelation also tells us where this army will come from.

> *The sixth angel poured out his bowl on the great river, the Euphrates; and its water was dried up, so that the way would be prepared for the kings from the east.*
>
> —Revelation 16:12

An army that large, two hundred million strong, would need to come from a much bigger nation than any that existed when the apostle John wrote that passage under the inspiration of the Holy Spirit. In addition, an army that large could only be directed and controlled by advanced orbital satellites, like those we have today. No nation could be described as having such a large army, and a population to support it, until today's communist China was established. We can conclude that the phrase "kings from the East" is speaking of modern China and other smaller Asian allies.

But why would the "kings from the East" want to march their massive army to the Middle East? It is because, at some point during the final seven years described in Revelation and Daniel 9:27, the leaders of China will perceive weakness in the Antichrist. Russia will make its move but fail to stop the Antichrist as described in the book of Daniel:

> *"And at the end time the king of the South will wage war with him, and the king of the North will storm against him with chariots, horsemen, and with many ships; and he will enter countries, overflow*

> *them, and pass through. He will also enter the Beautiful Land, and many countries will fall; but these will be rescued out of his hand: Edom, Moab, and the foremost of the sons of Ammon. Then he will reach out with his hand against other countries, and the land of Egypt will not escape. But he will gain control over the hidden treasures of gold and silver, and over all the precious things of Egypt; and Libyans and Ethiopians will follow at his heels. But rumors from the East and from the North will terrify him, and he will go out with great wrath to eliminate and annihilate many. And he will pitch the tents of his royal pavilion between the seas and the beautiful Holy Mountain; yet he will come to his end, and no one will help him.*
>
> —DANIEL 11:40–45

With the voice of Genghis Kahn whispering in their ears, China will conclude that the time is right to take world domination away from the Antichrist. To do this, they will need to go where the Antichrist is reigning as "God" in the Temple in Jerusalem. The Antichrist will respond by gathering his allies to make a stand against the advancing horde:

And I saw coming out of the mouth of the dragon, and out of the mouth of the beast, and out of the mouth of the false prophet, three unclean spirits like frogs; for they are spirits of demons, performing signs, which go out to the kings of the entire world, to gather them together for the war of the great day of God, the Almighty.

—REVELATION 16:13–14

And he gathered them together into a place called in the Hebrew tongue Armageddon.

—REVELATION 16:16 (KJV)

That's why Jesus said:

"For then shall be great tribulation, such as was not since the beginning of the world to this time, no, nor ever shall be. And except those days should be shortened, there should no flesh be saved: but for the elect's sake those days shall be shortened."

—MATTHEW 24:21–22 (KJV)

Just as the Battle of Armageddon is about to destroy the whole world:

> *"And then shall they see the Son of Man [Jesus] coming in a cloud with power and great glory."*
>
> —LUKE 21:27 (KJV)

Jesus will descend to the Mount of Olives outside Jerusalem and destroy the combined armies of China and the Antichrist, with a word:

> *From His mouth comes a sharp sword, so that with it He may strike down the nations, and He will rule them with a rod of iron; and He treads the wine press of the fierce wrath of God, the Almighty.*
>
> —REVELATION 19:15

> *Now this will be the plague with which the* LORD *will strike all the peoples who have gone to war against Jerusalem; their flesh will rot while they stand on their feet, and their eyes will rot in their sockets, and their tongue will rot in their mouth.*
>
> —ZECHARIAH 14:12

Then, Jesus will rule the world in peace, including China:

And it shall come to pass in the last days, that the mountain of the LORD*'s house shall be established in the top of the mountains, and shall be exalted above the hills; and all nations shall flow unto it.*

And many people shall go and say, Come ye, and let us go up to the mountain of the LORD*, to the house of the God of Jacob; and he will teach us of his ways, and we will walk in his paths: for out of Zion shall go forth the law, and the word of the* LORD *from Jerusalem.*

And he shall judge among the nations, and shall rebuke many people: and they shall beat their swords into plowshares, and their spears into pruninghooks: nation shall not lift up sword against nation, neither shall they learn war any more.

—ISAIAH 2:2–4 (KJV)

6

The Age-Old Rivalry

 Pin #8: Modern Islam's Power

The American Interstate Highway System was completed by President Dwight D. Eisenhower in the 1950s. The result was an automobile boom. Similar highway systems around the world would now be built, because in America, interstate highways resulted in an explosion of commerce.

But an automobile boom meant that something else was also going to boom, namely, gasoline. Suddenly,

"Oil is King" became the slogan of investors. Certain oil companies, together known as "the Seven Sisters," soon dominated world financial markets. And who benefited most from doing business with the "Seven Sisters"? Muslim oil sheiks in the Middle East.

The eighth bowling pin in my analogy points to America, the pinsetter, destined by God to set up modern Islam's power, seemingly to its own detriment. But God had a plan.

To understand the context of *this* end times development, we have to go back to the story of Abraham in the Bible. Let's look at Genesis 16, which took place during the days when Abraham's name was Abram, and his wife Sarah's name was Sarai:

> *Now Sarai, Abram's wife, had not borne him a child, but she had an Egyptian slave woman whose name was Hagar. So Sarai said to Abram, "See now, the* Lord *has prevented me from bearing children. Please have relations with my slave woman; perhaps I will obtain children through her." And Abram listened to the voice of Sarai. And so after Abram had lived ten years in the land of Canaan,*

Abram's wife Sarai took Hagar the Egyptian, her slave woman, and gave her to her husband Abram as his wife. Then he had relations with Hagar, and she conceived; and when Hagar became aware that she had conceived, her mistress was insignificant in her sight. So Sarai said to Abram, "May the wrong done to me be upon you! I put my slave woman into your arms, but when she saw that she had conceived, I was insignificant in her sight. May the Lord *judge between you and me." But Abram said to Sarai, "Look, your slave woman is in your power; do to her what is good in your sight." So Sarai treated her harshly, and she fled from her presence.*

Now the angel of the Lord *found her by a spring of water in the wilderness, by the spring on the way to Shur. He said, "Hagar, Sarai's slave woman, from where have you come, and where are you going?" And she said, "I am fleeing from the presence of my mistress Sarai." So the angel of the* Lord *said to her, "Return to your mistress, and submit to her authority." The angel of the* Lord *also said to her, "I will greatly multiply your descendants*

> *so that they will be too many to count." The angel of the* Lord *said to her further, "Behold, you are pregnant, and you will give birth to a son; and you shall name him Ishmael"*
>
> —Genesis 16:1–11

Hagar was likely heading back to her homeland, Egypt, but the harsh desert conditions made it unlikely that she would have arrived at her destination. Instead, the angel of the Lord saved her life. Hagar did give birth to a son, and she named him Ishmael as the angel directed. His birth was significant since his descendants play an important role in world history and in the world today. Who are the descendants of Ishmael? The Arabs. Sarah eventually gave birth to Abraham's son who was named Isaac. Who are the descendants of Sarah's son, Isaac? The Jews. The rivalry between Hagar and Sarah became the rivalry between the Arabs and the Jews.

Let's fast-forward to centuries after Abraham lived. Who is it that would primarily live in the Promised Land of the Jews, the land of Israel, from 70 A.D. until the "times of the Gentiles" would finally be fulfilled in the twentieth century? The Arabs. And who would object most vehemently to the idea of having Jewish people return to that land? The Arabs. And why is this age-old rivalry something the world has not been able to ignore? It is because the world has become largely dependent on Middle Eastern oil, controlled by Muslim Arabs. But what nation caused the world to become largely dependent on Middle Eastern oil in the first place? The United States, through the invention of the automobile and the highway systems that led to its widespread use.

So, where is this rivalry headed? Does the Bible tell us how "Sarah versus Hagar" is eventually going to play out?

Let's look at this end times prediction in Isaiah 19. This is God speaking through the prophet Isaiah:

> *And the LORD will strike Egypt, striking but healing; so they will return to the LORD, and He will respond to their pleas and heal them.*
>
> *On that day there will be a road from Egypt to Assyria, and the Assyrians will come into Egypt and the Egyptians into Assyria; and the Egyptians will worship with the Assyrians.*

> *On that day Israel will be the third party to Egypt and Assyria, a blessing in the midst of the earth, whom the* Lord *of armies has blessed, saying, "Blessed is Egypt My people, and Assyria the work of My hands, and Israel My inheritance."*
>
> —Isaiah 19:22–25

I believe "the striking of Egypt," referred to above, has to do with conflicts that will accompany the final battle of Armageddon. But this "striking" will actually cause the most populous Muslim nation in the Middle East, Egypt, to come to faith in the God of Israel, along with other Muslim Arab nations, represented by the "Assyria" reference. In the end, after Armageddon and after the Second Coming, Sarah and Hagar will live together in peace.

Could it be that God predestined Ishmael, the Arabs, to be His "times of the Gentiles" placeholder over the Jews' Promised Land for almost two thousand years? Yes, that's a strong possibility. And it's possible that God chose America to empower Ishmael, so that the rivalry between the Arabs and the Jews would bring end times events to a head. But what about radical Islam? Yes, the angel of the Lord saved Hagar, but does God still love radical Muslim Arabs today even in the age of jihad?

If prophetic patriotism is about desiring to help America fulfill its prophetic purpose before Christ's return, I believe this must also include praying for our extremist Muslim enemies, and somehow helping bring about their salvation in Christ just as Jesus said in Matthew:

> *But I say to you, love your enemies and pray for those who persecute you.*
>
> —MATTHEW 5:44

> *Then He said to His disciples, "The harvest is plentiful, but the workers are few. Therefore, plead with the Lord of the harvest to send out workers into His harvest."*
>
> —MATTHEW 9:37–38

Just as He loved Hagar, God still loves Ishmael. And the day is going to come when the Scripture in Isaiah will be fulfilled and God will say:

> *"Blessed is Egypt My people, and Assyria the work of My hands, and Israel My inheritance."*
>
> —Isaiah 19:25

But if we should pray for our extremist Muslim enemies, what about our domestic political adversaries?

7

The Final Harvest

Pin #9: Grassroots Populism

Pin #10: World Evangelism

Speaking through prophets in the Bible, God promised that He would sometimes communicate using visions and dreams unlike the direct communication He had with Moses:

He said, "Now hear My words:
If there is a prophet among you,

I, the LORD, will make Myself known to him in a vision.
I will speak with him in a dream.
It is not this way for My servant Moses;
He is faithful in all My household;
With him I speak mouth to mouth,
That is, openly, and not using mysterious language,
And he beholds the form of the LORD.
So why were you not afraid
To speak against My servant, against Moses?"

—NUMBERS 12:6–8

But He also said that as the time for fulfillment of His prophecies grew closer, the meaning of more of the "mysterious language" would become clear. Beyond that, He promised that He would not do anything having to do with God-initiated movements in history without speaking about it *first* through His prophets, whether it was in the form of a riddle or not.

This is God speaking to the prophet Amos:

> *"Surely the LORD God will do nothing without revealing His plan to His servants the prophets."*
>
> —AMOS 3:7

So again, God stated that prophecy would sometimes be given using dreams and visions and mysterious language, and that His work in human history will somehow always be represented by biblical prophecy.

With that in mind, let's look again at something Jesus said to His disciples:

> *"Jerusalem will be trampled underfoot by the Gentiles until the times of the Gentiles are fulfilled."*
>
> —LUKE 21:24

Where are the prophecies in the Bible about the "times of the Gentiles"?

In the book of Revelation, Jesus Christ appeared to the aging apostle John and spoke to him. He started with a message to seven churches in the Roman province of Asia which is present-day Turkey. You can read the messages to the churches in Revelation, chapters 1–3. I believe that it was in this portion of Scripture that God fulfilled His promise to reveal His plan for the "times of the Gentiles" prophetically.

First, I believe the messages to those seven city-churches that existed in John's time were also meant to be messages for all churches across time. But beyond that, the messages to the specific churches in John's time comprise a sequential prophetic riddle that predicted the "times of the Gentiles" and what would occur.

Although all the messages are relevant, let's examine the message to the church in Philadelphia, the sixth church in the sequence. This was a message to that church, existing in John's time. But I believe it was also intended by Jesus to prophetically represent the evangelical period of Protestant Christianity that took place from the 1700s until the start of World War I, after which came the modern era.

It was during this time that a Christian movement we now call revivalism came about. The Protestant leaders of that time stressed the simplicity of the Gospel of Jesus and formed organizations to send out missionaries to proclaim it. They wanted to get back to the essence of what it meant to be "saved" by spreading the message that God loves the people in the world and that salvation depended on believing and receiving Him personally as stated in the book of John:

> *But as many as received Him, to them He gave the right to become children of God, to those who believe in His name.*
>
> —JOHN 1:12

> *For God so loved the world, that He gave His only Son, so that everyone who believes in Him will not perish, but have eternal life.*
>
> —JOHN 3:16

They focused on evangelism, which again is the intentional sharing of one's faith with someone else, so that others might also believe. At the peak of this period, there were revival meetings that resulted in "Great Awakenings." From out of these "Great Awakenings" came what we now call evangelical Christianity. The goal was simple: "Let's get people saved."

What follows are the words of Jesus to the church in Philadelphia through the apostle John. Keep in mind that in the first century, when this was written, most new Christians were Jews, and so the "synagogue of Satan" reference is speaking of certain Jews who were opposing other Jews who had come to believe in Jesus as the Messiah of Israel. Let's read:

> *"And to the angel of the church in Philadelphia write:*
>
> *He who is holy, who is true, who has the key of David, who opens and no one will shut, and who shuts and no one opens, says this:*
>
> *'I know your deeds. Behold, I have put before you an open door which no one can shut, because you have a little power, and have followed My word, and have not denied My name. Behold, I will make those of the synagogue of Satan, who say that they are Jews and are not, but lie—I will make them come and bow down before your feet, and make them know that I have loved you. Because you have kept My word of perseverance, I also will keep you from the hour of the testing, that hour which is about to come upon the whole world, to test those who live on the earth. I am coming quickly; hold*

> *firmly to what you have, so that no one will take your crown. The one who overcomes, I will make him a pillar in the temple of My God, and he will not go out from it anymore; and I will write on him the name of My God, and the name of the city of My God, the new Jerusalem, which comes down out of heaven from My God, and My new name.'*
>
> —Revelation 3:7–12

At that time, I believe the "synagogue of Satan" reference was being directed to Jews opposing other Jews evangelistically delivering the Gospel. But those words can also be prophetically directed today at those who are against the evangelistic spreading of the Gospel message while still calling themselves Christian. Some Protestant denominations over the years have prioritized traditional forms of worship, lowered biblical moral standards, and resisted revivalism. Just as some mainstream Jews rejected evangelistic Christian Jews in those days, some people in modern denominational churches today also reject their own evangelistic brothers and sisters. Jesus was saying that such resistance actually comes from the enemy.

But I believe there is something much more profound that Jesus' message to the church in Philadelphia is prophetically telling us: In God's wisdom, I believe *one nation* was always intended in God's plan to take the lead in setting up a final surge of world evangelism, leading up to the Second Coming. I believe in addition to this letter representing Jesus' approval regarding evangelistic revivalism in general, Jesus also intended for this letter to prophetically refer to the United States of America.

What is the name of the city out of which our founding documents were birthed? Philadelphia. That is not a coincidence. "The door that no one can shut," I believe, similarly refers primarily to the First Amendment within our Bill of Rights in the Constitution. Why? Because here's what it says:

> *Congress shall make no law respecting an establishment of religion, or prohibiting the free exercise thereof; or abridging the freedom of speech, or of the press; or the right of the people peaceably to assemble, and to petition the Government for a redress of grievances.*

I believe this First Amendment "open door" was enshrined in our founding documents by Jesus Himself, for His own prophetic purpose. Especially the following, as stated in Jesus' own words:

> *"This gospel of the kingdom shall be preached in all the world for a witness unto all nations; and then shall the end come."*
>
> —MATTHEW 24:14 (KJV)

Our Bill of Rights is an "open door that no one can shut" in the sense that our Constitution is enshrined as law, and is supposed to be the last word regarding what is legal. But what if those in authority just ignore our Constitution, and the people of our republic do nothing about it?

That's where grassroots populism comes. By this, I mean populism that seeks to preserve America as a truly Constitutional Republic through involvement in civic affairs.

Grassroots populism is crucial for the preservation of American liberty because we are seeing in our time that too many in leadership have become unwilling to preserve it, even though they have sworn to do so. And American liberty is crucial, in God's eyes, because it is, and has been, the "open door" for world evangelism.

The United States of America has been the number one nation for the sending out of Christian missionaries and for the funding of foreign indigenous churches. But we need to understand that, going forward, God is able to accomplish world evangelism with, or without, America.

And so, America has come to a fork in the road.

If grassroots populism takes hold in the near term, I believe the road ahead for America will look like this: First, a religious Great Awakening, the turning back of globalism, continued American protection of Israel, and worldwide evangelism. Then the rapture, the final return of globalism, the rise of the Antichrist, Armageddon, and the Second Coming. This road leads to the fulfillment of America's last days prophetic purpose.

But if grassroots populism does not take hold in the near term, I believe the road ahead for America will instead look like this: First, the end of our freedoms under the Bill of Rights, the socialist control of those who believe in global governance, the protection of Israel occurring apart from America, and worldwide evangelism also occurring apart from America. And then the rapture, the Antichrist, Armageddon, and the Second Coming. This road leads to the loss of America's last days prophetic purpose.

Which road will it be?

I hope and believe that America will turn to God and journey down the first road which includes another Great Awakening fulfilling its purpose. Yet, I know that it's possible America will turn away from the first road by accepting governmental policies that take away the rights of an independent church, the free exercise of religion, and the freedom of speech. If the freedom of the church to speak the Gospel is no longer an accepted right according to the government, America journeys down the second road, and its prophetic purpose is cast aside.

I will leave it to the theologians to figure out how predestination and free will can both be simultaneously true. In the meantime, it's time to take action.

Conclusion

The Ten Commandments of Prophetic Patriotism

Bowling takes place in a bowling alley. And the pinsetter that represents America is set up in a bowling alley with Ten Commandments posted on its wall. The first commandment is a nonnegotiable:

#1: Give Your Life to Jesus Christ

You might never have heard this approach to patriotism before. America as a free nation is a beacon to many in the world because its freedoms are ordained by God. Allegiance to America is important but not more important than allegiance to God. My prayer is that you will speak with God as if He was sitting across the table from you. That's exactly what Jesus invites you to do:

> *Behold, I stand at the door and knock; if anyone hears My voice and opens the door, I will come in to him and will dine with him, and he with Me.*
>
> —REVELATION 3:20

My hope is that you will speak with Him by praying these words to Him:

> *Lord Jesus, Son of the living God, I don't want my life's spiritual energy to be spent on something that will pass away. I want my life to count for You. You have sovereignly ordained that I should live in the very nation that can prophetically usher in the Second Coming of Christ. But long before that, You died on the cross to take the punishment I deserve for my sins. Then You rose from the grave on the third day to conquer death, so I could live forever with You in heaven. That's why I'm deciding today, once and for all, that I want*

to be a Christ-follower. So, come into my heart, Lord Jesus, and I will live through Your Spirit, all the days of my life. Amen.

#2: Get Involved in a Local Church

Find a church that believes the Bible *is* God's Word, not one that believes the Bible merely *contains* God's Word. Participate especially in your church's small group life, until you feel that you have a "family." We will need to take care of each other in the days ahead.

#3: Get Involved in Your Political Party Before the Next Election

Jesus said, "To whom much is given, from him much will be required" in Luke 12:48 (NKJV). The ability to have influence in a participatory democracy is a gift from God, over which we Christians have sometimes been poor stewards. The day of the Christian bystander is over. After all, Jesus said in Matthew 5:13 that we are the "salt of the earth." It's time to become an active part of the solution!

Learn about City Councils and County Commissioners. Investigate civic involvement at the precinct level. See what it takes to participate on election boards. Become a poll worker or vote-counting inspector. Don't be afraid to help get the word out about the candidate with which you agree. Do not be ashamed to attend political gatherings espousing causes in which you believe.

#4: Attend Local School Board Meetings

Our children are precious. Investigate what's being taught in your local public schools. Understand that if you pay taxes, the local school staff and Board of Education work for you. Some of you might even feel led by God to run for a school board position.

#5: Phone or Email your Elected Representatives

Let your voice be heard. Constituent responses to ongoing questions and issues are measured. Congressional votes on legislation are changed by calls and emails. Don't be silent!

#6: Find Alternative News Sources

Citizen journalism is resurrecting the freedom of the press every day in America. Today, breaking news by nontraditional news sources is exerting as much influence as that which takes place in the mainstream. Find a source of news that truthfully explores current events. Ideally, find more than one. At the same time, I also recommend that you keep abreast of what's being said by news sources that you do not trust. Weigh the messaging and ask for discernment from God to know the truth.

#7: Find Alternative Social Media

Big Tech as it currently exists may eventually be broken up, but now is the time to find platforms that embrace a spirit of freedom. Canceling the messengers of truth has always been the enemy's way, but the true purpose behind limiting free speech is often overlooked. The inroad created by canceling political discourse is actually a precursor to canceling the spread of the Gospel of Jesus Christ. However, as we discussed in an earlier chapter, that is ultimately not going to succeed.

#8: Support Targeted Businesses and Avoid Businesses That Target You

Many prophetic patriots who own businesses will become targets in the days ahead. Whenever this happens, it is imperative that the Christian community support them financially. After all, the people with the ability to bring in significant income through their products are crucial to the spreading of the Gospel! By supporting them, you can help to spread the Gospel of Jesus Christ around the world!

In addition to this, it goes without saying that you should not support, with God's money, businesses that openly oppose God.

#9: Vote... and Don't Give Up Despite Setbacks!

In a divided nation, every vote counts. It will still count when it is not as divided as it is now. No matter what ends up happening with regard to mail-in voting, always vote in person unless you are physically not able to do so. And if possible, seek to be able to verify your vote after the fact, especially when it comes to national elections. Beyond this, do everything you can to support accurate voter rolls, election-process transparency, and election integrity.

#10: Pray

Pray for America. Pray that God's prophetic purpose for this nation will be achieved to the fullest extent that God intended! Pray for courage. We must all rise to the occasion, no matter what those who oppose us may say or do. Getting involved is not a threat to democracy, it *is* democracy. Pray for our political adversaries and forgive them. There may be people on the other side who will change their heart and mind to become a hero for the Constitution of the United States and the Gospel of Jesus Christ. So, pray for the worst of them, as the early church prayed for Saul of Tarsus before he became the apostle Paul. And finally, if you feel so led, pray for me and my family as we endeavor to proclaim the Good News of Jesus Christ, and America's Prophetic Purpose.

About the Author

Dominic Francese is a pastor, chaplain, and Bible teacher. His master of divinity degree is from Regent University in Virginia Beach. He is licensed by the Missionary Church, USA, and has been ordained by the Christian & Missionary Alliance. To communicate with Dominic Francese, visit www.propheticpatriotism.com.